The Little Shepherd Girl

A CHRISTMAS STORY

BY Juliann Henry

ILLUSTRATED BY Jim Madsen

David C Cook®

transforming little lives together

To my daughter, Sara, created in the
image of God and beloved by Jesus.
–*J.H.*

To my three little shepherds
Mckenzie, Hannah & Easton.
Always Believe.
–*J.M.*

THE LITTLE SHEPHERD GIRL
Published by David C. Cook
4050 Lee Vance View
Colorado Springs, CO 80918 U.S.A.

David C. Cook Distribution Canada
55 Woodslee Avenue, Paris, Ontario, Canada N3L 3E5

David C. Cook U.K., Kingsway Communications
Eastbourne, East Sussex BN23 6NT, England

David C. Cook and the graphic circle C logo are registered trademarks of Cook Communications Ministries.

ISBN 978-0-7814-4513-9

Text copyright © 2007 by Juliann Henry
Illustrations © 2007 Jim Madsen

Printed in South Korea
First Printing 2007

1 2 3 4 5 6 7 8 9 10

Author's Note

From the earliest days, boys and girls have served as shepherds, caring for their family's sheep. David was a shepherd before he became king of Israel (*1 Samuel 16:11*). Rachel was a shepherd before she married Jacob, Isaac's son (*Genesis 29:9*). Contemporary stereotypes that only portray male shepherds fail to understand that in primitive pastoral societies, both women and men actively cared for valuable livestock, the income source for nomadic families. A traditional Mexican nativity set always includes two shepherd figures: one a boy and the other a girl. *–J.H.*

"If God meant all the stars to shine exactly the same, then why did he make so many?"

Sarah asked her father, but her father didn't know.

Sarah asked her mother, but she was too busy with Sarah's six younger sisters to think about such big questions.

Sarah asked an easier question.

"Tonight, Father? May I go out into the field with the flock tonight?"

Sarah's father did not know the answer to that question either; Sarah was always asking questions he could not answer. He looked at Sarah's mother, and they talked with their eyes.

"No, Sarah," he finally said. "Daughters are meant for weaving and baking flat cakes. Only sons can protect the flock from a hungry wolf. That is just the way of things."

"But, Father," Sarah's voice rose, "you have no sons to bring the sheep to pasture! And why does my nose prefer the smell of sweet clover to that of bread dough?"

"I don't know, Sarah. I don't know."

Not long after, Sarah made herself a shepherd's crook and fashioned a bag out of leather. She woke up early in the morning so she could go out into the field to practice shepherding before chores.

But each morning, her father walked to the top of the big hill and called out, "Time to come home, Sarah. The bread is not baked, the weaving not done."

Sarah's feet made little puffs of dust as she walked home. "Father, if I were a star in the night sky I would shine on the lambs all night."

Sarah's father scratched his chin. After a long pause he said, "Daughter, I will miss you when you go out into the fields. You will sleep with your cousins tonight, guarding the flock."

Sarah began to leap and dance. "Really, Father? You mean it?"

"Yes, child. Now come! Let's go tell your mother."

It was a long walk to the fields where Sarah's cousins kept the sheep, but she didn't mind. She skipped the whole way.

Sarah worked hard that night! No one could deny it. Her cousins let her do most of the work. They simply could not stop her. After the sheep were bedded down the boys sent Sarah to gather wood for the evening fire.

Sarah was deep in the field when an amazing thing happened. The sky let go of its stars and they flew down to earth.

Sarah saw all this from a distance.

She heard whirring and rustling wind and then singing. She saw her terrified cousins fall to the ground as the stars came to rest before them. And then she heard the stars speak.

Gloria! Peace on earth!

Angels! Sarah couldn't believe her eyes. What were they saying?

Fear not! There's good news! Today a Savior is born—Christ the Lord! Go into town and see him—wrapped in cloth, in a manger.

Sarah frantically waded through the flock to join the other shepherds, but every time she took a step, a sheep blocked her path. By the time she reached the fire, the angels were gone. So were her cousins. They had run off to see the Savior.

In their great excitement they had forgotten all about her.

A good shepherd would not abandon her sheep. This Sarah knew.

Oh, what baaa-ing and bleating could be heard as Sarah and all the sheep headed down the path and into town.

The noise of the lambs echoed off the houses. The mules lining the streets brayed nervously as lambs ran past their legs. People peered out of windows to see what was going on.

Sarah called to those she saw, "Have you seen a baby in a manger?" Those who heard her laughed at the silliness of her question. But most could not make out her words over the great noise of the sheep.

The flock wandered from one end of town to the other, their hooves kicking dust in the air.

Why hadn't her cousins waited for her? There must be a hundred mangers in town! How could she possibly find the right one?

Just then the sheep rounded a bend, and came to a sudden stop—a dead end. Helpless, Sarah stood in the darkness. It would be too difficult to turn the sheep around by herself. Tears stung her eyes as she looked up at the brilliant night sky.

It was then that Sarah noticed something: one star, brighter than the rest. It seemed so close that she could almost touch it. It hung over the stable at the far end of the street.

Sarah called to the sheep to follow her. Some did. Some did not. No matter. They were safe where they were. Sarah crept to the stable and peered inside.

Through the opening she saw a man and a woman and something else: a small form wiggling in a manger. It began to cry. The woman picked up the baby to comfort him.

The man looked up, startled by a young girl at the door and the sounds of a hundred restless sheep. "Yours?" he asked.

"Yes," Sarah answered wearily. "But they're stuck."

"Come and see the baby. Then I'll help you with your sheep," said the man.

Sarah was sitting on a clump of hay, holding a tiny baby fist, when her cousins arrived. "How? H-how'd you get here before us?" they asked. "And with all the sheep!"

"I followed the sheep into town," said Sarah. "But then I got lost. I saw the star. It led me here."

The man chuckled, "Never before has a baby seen so many animals on the day of his birth. It will be a wonder if he doesn't grow up to be a shepherd himself!"

Dawn broke over the hills as Sarah headed home, tired but excited from her very first night with the flock. God had done a new thing, a wonderful thing, right in Bethlehem. Sarah couldn't wait to tell her father, mother and younger sisters.

Later that evening Sarah walked with her father out into the field. They talked about the angels good news.

Sarah pointed to the stars, too many to count, and said, "Father see those? They all look the same, but some are different. Some have the job of flying to earth to tell about a Savior."

"And some," her father said tenderly, "are sent by a loving Father to lead a little shepherd girl home to him."

THE SHEPHERDS RETURNED, GLORIFYING AND PRAISING GOD FOR ALL THE THINGS THEY HAD HEARD AND SEEN, WHICH WERE JUST AS THEY HAD BEEN TOLD.   Luke 2:20